DK findout!
Rome

Author and consultant: Peter Chrisp

Penguin Random House

Senior editor Marie Greenwood
Senior art editor Jim Green
Editor Olivia Stanford
Design assistant Rhea Gaughan
Additional design Helen Garvey
Managing editor Laura Gilbert
Managing art editor Diane Peyton Jones
Pre-production producer Dragana Puvacic
Senior producer Charlotte Oliver
Art director Martin Wilson
Publisher Sarah Larter
Publishing director Sophie Mitchell

Educational consultant Jacqueline Harris

First published in Great Britain in 2016
This paperback edition first published in 2017 by
Dorling Kindersley Limited
80 Strand, London, WC2R 0RL

A CIP catalogue record for this book
is available from the British Library.
ISBN: 978-0-2413-3137-8

Printed and bound in China

A WORLD OF IDEAS:
SEE ALL THERE IS TO KNOW

www.dk.com

BCE/CE
When you see the letters BCE, it means years
Before the Common Era, which began in the
year 1CE (Common Era).

Contents

Temple

Citizen

Theatrical masks

Roman coin

Freedwoman

Legionary

Julius Caesar

Roman tweezers and ear scoop

Who were the Romans?

Let's travel back in time, almost 2,000 years, to the Roman Empire. The year is 117CE, and the Empire is at its greatest size, ruled by Emperor Trajan. Let's talk to these two Romans, playwright Terentius and his wife, and ask them about their world.

Q: What is an empire and where is it?

A: An empire is a large area of land ruled by one person. The Roman Empire covers most of Europe and beyond.

Q: What is the capital city of the Empire?

A: The great city of Rome! It is built on the Tiber river in Italia. To us, it's the centre of the world.

Q: Have you always had an emperor?

A: No. Until 27BCE, Rome was a republic, ruled by a government voted for by the people. Before that it was ruled by kings.

Q: How did you get to have such a big empire?

A: We conquered it with our armies. We are good at winning wars!

Over **20 per cent** of the world's population were part of the Roman Empire at its height.

A: The first king of Rome was Romulus. It was said he built Rome after killing his twin brother, Remus, in an argument over where to put it. He then named the city after himself.

Q: Why are you called Romans?

A: Wherever we rule, people now dress like us, use the same coins, and some worship our gods. But we often add their gods to our own.

Q: Have you Romans changed the lands you conquered?

A: Today, it stretches 4,000 km (2,500 miles) east to west and 3,700 km (2,300 miles) north to south. About 60 million people live in it.

Q: How big is the Roman Empire?

Roman society

Within the Roman Empire, there were different groups of people, with different rights, or entitlements. Roman citizens had more rights than non-citizens, and slaves had no rights at all. However, slaves could earn their freedom, and rise to a different level in society. The way people dressed helped show which group they belonged to.

Stola
This ankle-length dress, called a stola, was worn by married women.

White toga
The toga was a woollen robe, draped around the body.

Tunic
This slave is wearing a simple tunic.

Palla
A palla (shawl) was worn over the stola.

Slave
Slaves were people who were owned by other Romans as property. They might be prisoners captured in war, or the children of slave parents. As the Empire became bigger, so did the number of slaves.

Freedwoman
Through loyal service, slaves could earn their freedom. Former slaves were called freedmen and freedwomen. They kept close ties with their former owners, who might set them up in business, such as shopkeeping.

Citizen
The rights of a Roman citizen included being able to vote, to serve as a government official, and to wear a long woollen robe called a toga.

Head wreath
Instead of a crown, emperors sometimes wore a wreath of laurel leaves. Sometimes the wreath was made of gold.

Purple toga
Emperors wore a purple and gold toga when they appeared in public.

Emperor

From 27 BCE, Rome was ruled by an all-powerful emperor. He was high priest, lawmaker, and army commander-in-chief. After he died, he might even be worshipped as a god, as was the case with Emperor Augustus.

Toga colours

There were several types of toga. Each kind was worn at particular times or occasions, or by different classes of citizen.

Toga pura
This toga was made of plain wool. It was the everyday toga of ordinary citizens.

Toga picta
This purple and gold toga was worn by emperors.

Toga candida
A toga whitened with chalk was worn by men standing for election.

Toga pulla
A dark brown toga was worn by men in mourning for a person who had died.

Toga praetexta
The toga praetexta was plain with a purple border. It was worn by high officials.

Britannia (Britain)

Emperor Claudius invaded Britannia in 43CE, but only part of the island was ever won.

Warrior Briton
The Celtic warriors of Britain painted themselves with patterns before going into battle.

Londinium •

Italia (Italy)

It took a hundred years of warfare before Rome conquered the whole of Italy, in 264BCE.

Roman soldier
Roman foot soldiers were called legionaries.

Gallia (Gaul)

Gallia was conquered by Julius Caesar in 58–50BCE. Before the invasion it wasn't united, but ruled by separate Celtic tribes.

Gallic warrior
Warriors from the Celtic tribes were led by a chieftain.

• Rome

Pompeii •

Carthaginian Empire

Carthage was a powerful city on the coast of the Mediterranean. Between 264–146BCE, Rome fought and won three wars against Carthage.

War elephant
Some Carthaginians fought from the backs of war elephants.

• Carthage

The Roman Empire

This map shows how the Roman Empire grew in size, through wars of conquest, between 146BCE and 117CE. It included all the lands around the Mediterranean Sea, which the Romans were able to call "mare nostrum", meaning "our sea". Before 27BCE, Rome was ruled by elected officials, but after it was controlled by emperors.

Graecia (Greece)

The Romans conquered the Greeks in 146BCE. Yet they admired their way of life, copying Greek buildings, art, and sciences.

Greek soldier
Soldiers from Greece fought with long spears called sarissas.

Parthian Empire

The Parthians ruled a rival empire to the east. Although the emperor Trajan conquered part of their empire, in 115–117CE, they later won it back.

KEY

The purple areas represent the lands the Romans ruled. The areas in lighter purples were conquered later than the darker areas.

The Republic, 146BCE, following the conquest of Greece and Carthage.

Early Empire, 27BCE, when the first emperor Augustus came to power.

The Empire, 117CE, under the emperor Trajan the Empire reached its greatest extent.

Parthian soldier
Parthians fought as heavily armoured horsemen.

Constantinople

Athens

Mediterranean Sea

Alexandria

Roman Empire, shown in purple, on a map of the world.

Ruler of Rome

Julius Caesar was a great soldier and general. Before the emperors were in charge, the Senate, a group of noblemen, ruled Rome. In 44BCE Caesar defeated the Senate and made himself "Dictator". Here, we imagine how an interview with Julius Caesar may have gone.

Caesar's head
Julius Caesar was the first living Roman to have his portrait on a coin.

Q: Caesar, which of your conquests are you most proud of?

A: It's very hard to choose between them. As I always say "veni, vidi, vici".

Q: "I came, I saw, I conquered"?

A: Exactly. You should really read the book I wrote about my success in Gaul. I also led two expeditions across the sea to Britain.

Q: Is it true that the Britons paint themselves blue?

A: Yes, when they go into battle. But we Romans will show them the proper way to live. We'll make sure that one day, they will even have bathhouses!

Q: Why did you go to war with the Senate, Caesar?

A: After successfully conquering Gaul (France) they ordered me to give up my army, and return to Rome as a private citizen. I couldn't do that, could I?

Q: How did you defeat the Senate?

A: I am the best general Rome has. My loyal soldiers, toughened up by fighting those Gauls, are unbeatable. The Senate's leader Pompey was no match for me.

Q: People say that you've started acting like a king.

A: I am not a king, but the Empire needs a strong leader to keep it united.

Q: Why have you put your portraits on coins?

A: The people need to know who is in charge. Don't I deserve the honour, after all I've done for Rome?

Statue of Caesar
This is a bronze statue of Caesar dressed in military clothing.

I came, I saw, I conquered!

Q: Which are your greatest achievements?

A: I created a new calendar so a year now has 365 days. Before, there were only 355 and an extra month had to be added every few years. A month has been renamed "Julius" (July) in my honour.

Q: Aren't you worried about making enemies?

A: I'm good at winning over enemies. I forgave Brutus, who fought against me in the civil war. Now he's like a son to me!

Q: What are your plans for the future?

A: In three days, I set off east, to conquer the Parthians of Persia. Today I have a meeting with the senators at the Theatre of Pompey. I'm just off to see dear Brutus there now.

Dagger

Stabbed

Caesar never got to fight the Parthians. In 44BCE, on the 15 March, a day known as the "Ides of March", Caesar was killed. He was stabbed to death by a group of senators led by his former friend Brutus.

The emperors

A Roman emperor had enormous power. Some emperors used their powers wisely, while others were just not up to the job. Here are four of them. Were they good or bad leaders?

Augustus

After defeating his rivals, Augustus made himself the first emperor in 27BCE. He had total power, but did not live like a king, claiming that he was just the "first citizen".

Good

- Brought peace and firm rule, after years of civil war.

- Lived simply, unlike a very rich and powerful ruler.

- Expanded the Empire.

- Built many fine public buildings and good roads.

- Funded the arts, such as literature.

Bad

- Took power by force, killing his rivals.

Verdict: Good

Nero

Nero ruled well at first: encouraging art and culture, and boosting trade. But power went to his head. Nero murdered anyone who challenged him, including his own mother!

Good

- Gave many splendid public shows to entertain the people.

- Built theatres, and set up athletic games and chariot races.

Bad

- Had anyone who did not agree with him put to death.

- Murdered his mother, wife, and step-brother.

- Was rumoured to have started the Great Fire of Rome in 64CE.

- Blamed Christians for the Great Fire.

- After the Great Fire, he took over a large area of Rome to build a huge palace (the Golden House) just for himself!

Verdict: Bad

FACT FILE

» **Born:**
53CE

» **Ruled:**
98–117CE

» **Fun fact:** Born in
Spain, he was the first
non-Roman emperor.

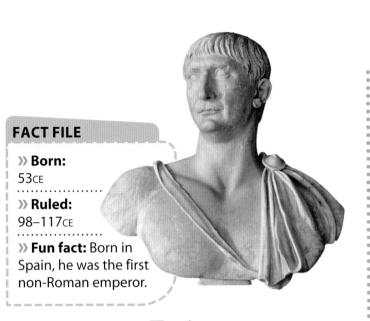

Trajan

Trajan was a great general, whose success
and popularity led to him being adopted by
the emperor Neva. Trajan's conquests saw
the Empire expand to its maximum size.

Good

- Expanded the
  Empire.

- Built a new forum in
  Rome, using money
  he won in war.

- Provided funding
  to help educate
  orphans and poor
  children in Rome.

- Reduced taxes.

Bad

- His expansion of the
  Empire made it so
  big that it became
  hard to rule well.

- Forced thousands of
  prisoners of war to
  fight as gladiators.

FACT FILE

» **Born:**
76CE

» **Ruled:**
117–138CE

» **Fun fact:** He ordered
Rome's biggest building
project: Hadrian's Wall.

Hadrian

Hadrian, who followed Trajan, gave up some
of the Empire's earlier conquests in order to
strengthen the Empire's borders. He was
possibly the hardest working emperor.

Good

- A very good
  administrator, he
  made the Empire
  more secure.

- Built strong frontier
  defences, such as
  Hadrian's Wall to stop
  the northern tribes
  attacking Britannia.

- Travelled widely
  around the Empire.

- A cultured man, he
  wrote poetry and
  designed buildings.

- Built many new public
  buildings and rebuilt
  others, including the
  Pantheon.

Bad

- His travels meant he
  was often away from
  Rome, making him
  unpopular there.

- Executed several
  senators who had
  plotted against him,
  and then denied it!

**Verdict:
Good**

**Verdict:
Good**

Roman army

The Roman army was made up of around 28 legions, each with about 5,000 soldiers, or legionaries, who fought on foot. They were helped by auxiliaries, who were fighters from lands conquered by the Romans. They brought extra skills that the legionaries may not have had, and included cavalrymen, archers, and slingers.

Slingers

Slinger auxiliaries could fire stones at the enemy with deadly accuracy. They came from islands southeast of Spain, where boys were trained to use a sling from a very early age.

Leather bag for carrying stones

Ways of fighting

Legionaries grouped themselves in various different ways when fighting, in order to give themselves the best possible protection and to help them attack the enemy more effectively.

Testudo
These soldiers are grouped into a testudo (Latin for "tortoise"). Holding shields over their heads gives the men a hard, protective "shell", just like a tortoise!

Bare shins
Only the lower legs, or shins, of the legionaries were left unprotected.

Vexillum
This flag-like banner was used to rally the men in battle, helping them to stay together. Vexillum means "little sail".

Standard bearer
This legionary's task was the most dangerous, as he has no shield to protect him from enemy fire.

Curved shield
The large, curved shape wraps around the legionary's body.

Army organization

Legions were broken up into smaller units, called cohorts and centuries. This made it easier to manage such a large group of men. Each cohort or century had its own leader.

 = 1 legionary

80 legionaries

Century
A century consisted of 80 men. They were commanded by an army officer called a centurion.

 = 1 century

6 centuries

Cohort
A cohort was made up of six centuries grouped together, making 480 soldiers in all. They were led by a more senior centurion than the ones in charge of each century.

 = 1 cohort

10 cohorts

Legion
As well as 10 cohorts of foot soldiers, there were around 120 horsemen, who acted as messengers and scouts. The commander of a legion was appointed by the emperor, and was called a legatus.

 = 1 legion

Roman soldiers

Roman foot-soldiers, called legionaries, had full-time jobs in the army. They were highly trained, well-armed, and always ready for battle. Lots of exercise, such as running and swimming, kept them fighting fit. This made the Roman army the most feared in the ancient world.

Legionary

Legionaries all wore the same clothing and had the same equipment. This helped them fight together as a group. They were led by a centurion.

Helmet
A helmet, with cheek flaps to protect the face, covered most of the head, but let the soldier see and hear clearly.

Armour
A legionary's body armour was made of overlapping metal strips, which allowed him to move and bend freely.

Sword
A short sword, called a gladius, was kept in a scabbard, or cover, on the right hip. It was used for stabbing.

Shield
A long curved wooden shield, with a central bronze boss (plate), protected most of the legionary's body.

Sandals
Leather sandals had soles lined with iron studs, to stop them wearing out on long marches.

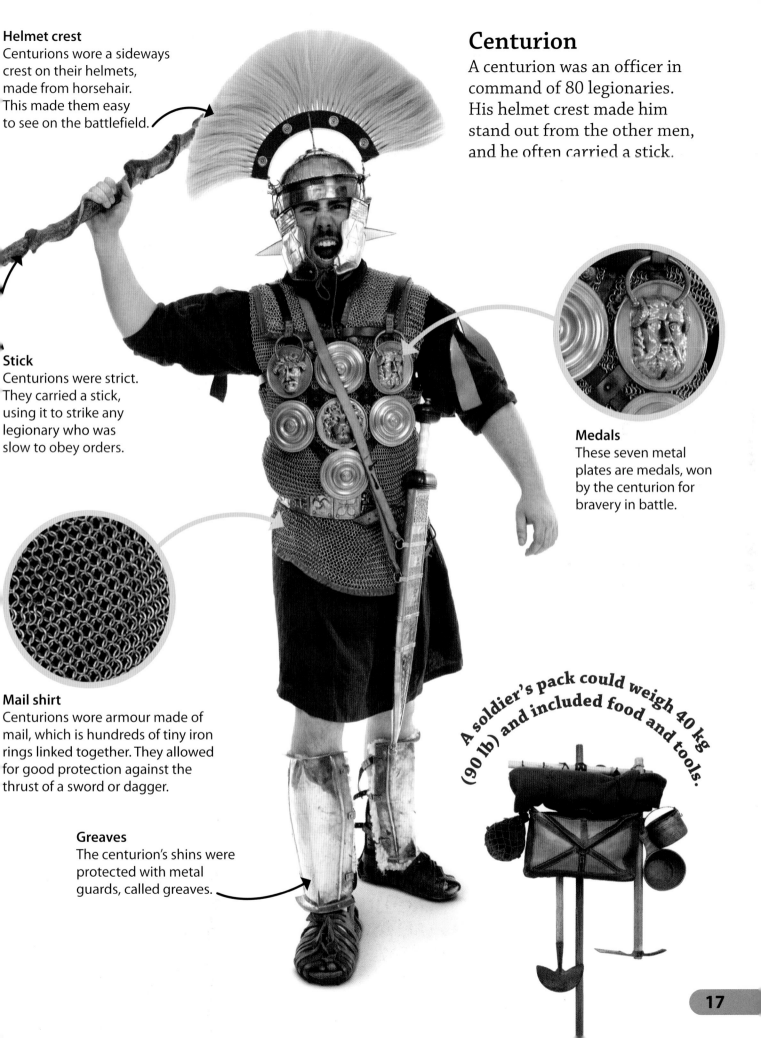

Helmet crest
Centurions wore a sideways crest on their helmets, made from horsehair. This made them easy to see on the battlefield.

Centurion

A centurion was an officer in command of 80 legionaries. His helmet crest made him stand out from the other men, and he often carried a stick.

Stick
Centurions were strict. They carried a stick, using it to strike any legionary who was slow to obey orders.

Medals
These seven metal plates are medals, won by the centurion for bravery in battle.

Mail shirt
Centurions wore armour made of mail, which is hundreds of tiny iron rings linked together. They allowed for good protection against the thrust of a sword or dagger.

Greaves
The centurion's shins were protected with metal guards, called greaves.

A soldier's pack could weigh 40 kg (90 lb) and included food and tools.

At work

Although the Romans lived 2,000 years ago, many of the jobs they did are still done by people today. What job do you think you would have done if you lived in Roman times?

Baker

Romans usually bought their bread from a bakery. The loaves were baked in a round oven. Roman bakers were also millers. They ground grain into flour, using mills powered by donkeys or horses.

Actor

Romans loved the theatre, especially as it was free! Actors performed on a semi-circular stage. Some actors were big stars, with devoted fans, just like today. However, unlike modern actors, they usually wore masks. These showed what the character was feeling, for example happiness, sadness, fear, or surprise.

Roman theatre in Bosra, Syria

Engineer

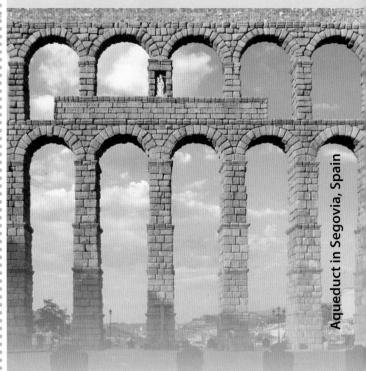

Aqueduct in Segovia, Spain

Roman engineers, who designed buildings like this aqueduct, were highly skilled. Aqueducts were used to channel water to towns and cities. The aqueduct had to be built at exactly the right angle to ensure the water flowed smoothly.

Lawyer

Let justice be your cause!

Roman lawyers had to make long speeches, to persuade people to see their point of view. Lawyers either accused or defended people brought to trial for crimes, such as theft or murder. Many speeches by Roman lawyers can still be read today.

Teacher

Roman teachers ran schools, which were just for boys. Lessons usually took place in the teacher's own home. Teachers used a tablet made of wax and a pointed stick, called a stylus, to teach children how to write.

Doctor

Roman doctors used instruments that are still in use today, such as sharp scalpels for cutting and forceps (tweezers) for removing splinters. The Romans believed that gods could help them get well, so doctors combined practical skills with religious rituals.

Surgeon's knife

Surgical forceps

Farmer

In Roman times, most people lived in the countryside, and worked as farmers. Much of the hard work, such as raising animals and growing crops, was done by slaves.

Shopkeeper

Shops were found on the ground floor of houses and sold everything. Even takeaway food was available! In 107–110CE, the emperor Trajan built a shopping centre with more than 150 shops.

A

Frying pan

This Roman soldier's frying pan has a folding handle. This meant that it could be easily packed away into his baggage or stored for later use.

B

Razor

Roman barbers shaved their customers using a razor. This had to be regularly resharpened on a piece of leather called a strop.

C

Sponge stick

Toilet paper had not been invented in Roman times. Instead, people used a sea sponge on a long stick.

Everyday things

While life in Roman times was very different from how we live our lives today, some things were similar. Here's a collection of items that people used in Roman times. Some of them you may recognize, while others may seem strange. See if you can match each item with its description.

D
Plumb line
To work out if a wall or doorway was straight, Roman builders used a plumb line. This is a lead weight dangled on a length of string.

E
Folding tool
This folding device, like a pen knife, combines a spoon, knife, and other tools. It may have belonged to a traveller, such as a merchant.

F
Strigil
Instead of soap, Romans rubbed themselves with olive oil, and then scraped their skin clean with a curved metal tool, called a strigil.

Public toilet
Roman towns had public toilets, where people sat side by side! They were flushed by flowing water. Water also flowed through a channel on the floor and sponges were rinsed in this after use, and then left for the next visitor.

I'm not sure about her. She looks like the lazy type to me…

Buying a slave

You could buy a slave in the marketplace, just like you would buy any other goods you wanted. A buyer would look very carefully at the slaves on sale, checking for signs of carelessness, laziness, a bad temper, or poor health.

Slaves

Slaves were men, women, and children who were owned as property. If they disobeyed their owner, they might be harshly punished. Most Romans saw nothing wrong in owning slaves. However, many believed that they had a duty to treat their slaves well.

WOW!

! Some slaves wore **tags** saying who owned them, in case they **ran away.**

A runaway slave would be returned to the address on the tag.

Slaves served food and wine at mealtimes.

A trusted slave delivered letters and ran errands.

Changing roles

A special holiday for slaves was held every year in late December. This was during the Saturnalia festival, which honoured Saturn, the father of Jupiter. For one day, slaves swapped places with their owners, who served them.

Some owners treated their slaves to a special feast.

Slaves at work

Rich Romans had slaves to do almost everything for them. Slaves helped their master or mistress to dress in the morning and to get ready for bed at night. Slaves also prepared and served all their meals, cleaned up after them, and even entertained them.

A female slave would dress a Roman lady's hair.

You have served me well. I therefore give you your freedom.

Wow! Now, I can buy my own slave!

Freeing a slave

Slaves who were loyal and worked hard might be rewarded by being given their freedom. Many slaves were highly skilled and, once they were free, went on to run successful businesses and even have their own slaves.

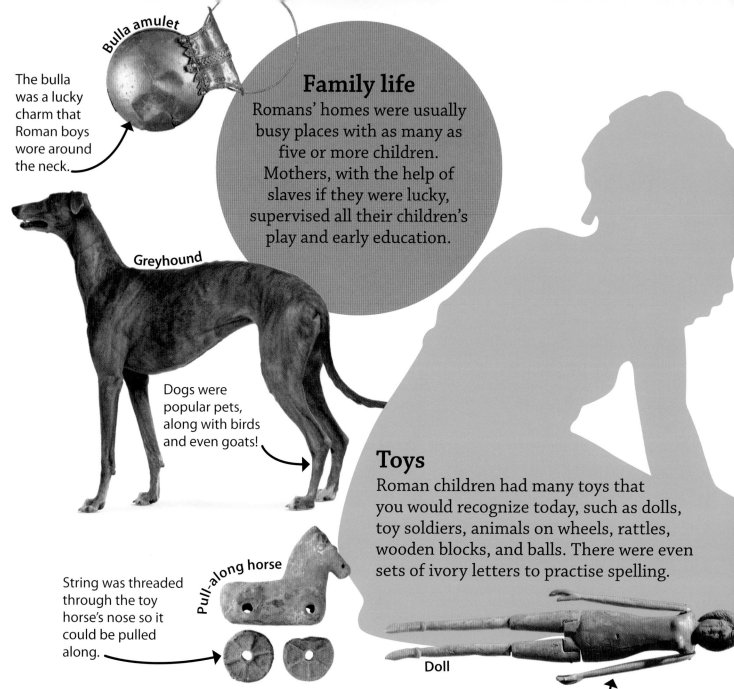

Bulla amulet

The bulla was a lucky charm that Roman boys wore around the neck.

Family life

Romans' homes were usually busy places with as many as five or more children. Mothers, with the help of slaves if they were lucky, supervised all their children's play and early education.

Greyhound

Dogs were popular pets, along with birds and even goats!

Toys

Roman children had many toys that you would recognize today, such as dolls, toy soldiers, animals on wheels, rattles, wooden blocks, and balls. There were even sets of ivory letters to practise spelling.

Pull-along horse

String was threaded through the toy horse's nose so it could be pulled along.

Doll

Girls played with dolls, made from wood or bone. This one has moveable arms and legs.

Children in Rome

Roman children were very much like children are today. At home, they had toys, played games, and kept pets. Some of them also went to school, although it was very rare for a girl to go. Many children, especially from rich families, were educated at home, taught by either their parents, slaves, or hired tutors.

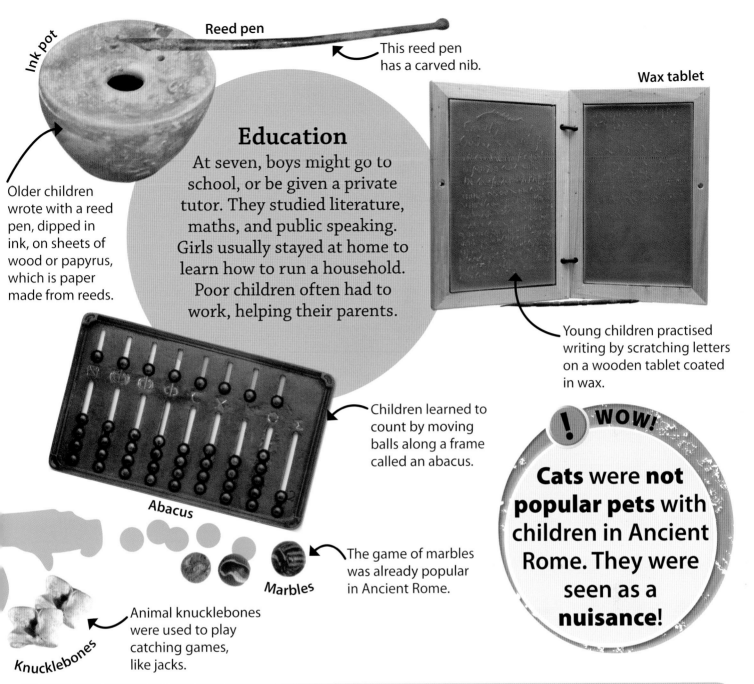

Ink pot

Reed pen

This reed pen has a carved nib.

Older children wrote with a reed pen, dipped in ink, on sheets of wood or papyrus, which is paper made from reeds.

Wax tablet

Education

At seven, boys might go to school, or be given a private tutor. They studied literature, maths, and public speaking. Girls usually stayed at home to learn how to run a household. Poor children often had to work, helping their parents.

Young children practised writing by scratching letters on a wooden tablet coated in wax.

Children learned to count by moving balls along a frame called an abacus.

Abacus

The game of marbles was already popular in Ancient Rome.

Marbles

! WOW!

Cats were **not popular pets** with children in Ancient Rome. They were seen as a **nuisance!**

Animal knucklebones were used to play catching games, like jacks.

Knucklebones

Home schooling

Rich Romans usually hired tutors to teach their children at home. Here two teenage boys are seen reading to their tutor. A third boy looks like he has just arrived, possibly a little late for his lesson!

Carving showing a Roman lesson, from Germany.

Roman clothing

The Romans did not wear close-fitting tailored clothes, such as jackets or trousers. Clothes for men and women were made of large pieces of cloth, draped around the body or tied with belts. The basic item was the tunic, made from two rectangles of fabric with two holes for the arms. It was knee length for men, and longer for women.

Women's clothing

On top of their tunic, women wore an ankle-length dress, called a stola. Over this a shawl, called a palla, could be added. The palla might rest on the shoulders or cover the head, like a veil.

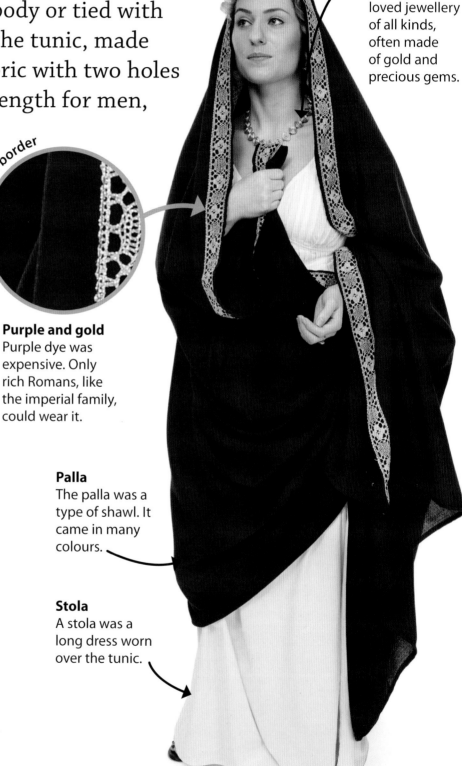

Gold border

Necklace
Roman women loved jewellery of all kinds, often made of gold and precious gems.

Purple and gold
Purple dye was expensive. Only rich Romans, like the imperial family, could wear it.

Palla
The palla was a type of shawl. It came in many colours.

Stola
A stola was a long dress worn over the tunic.

! WOW!

Emperor Augustus, who felt the cold, wore **four tunics** at the same time!

Men's clothing

Male citizens had the right to wear a toga, a woollen sheet draped around the body. This was so important to Romans that they called themselves "the race that wears the toga".

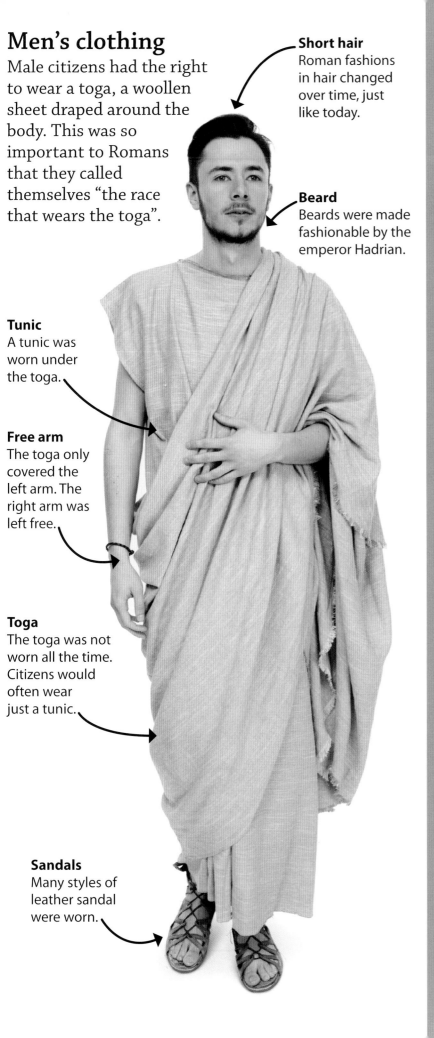

Short hair
Roman fashions in hair changed over time, just like today.

Beard
Beards were made fashionable by the emperor Hadrian.

Tunic
A tunic was worn under the toga.

Free arm
The toga only covered the left arm. The right arm was left free.

Toga
The toga was not worn all the time. Citizens would often wear just a tunic.

Sandals
Many styles of leather sandal were worn.

Putting on a toga

Usually a slave would help a Roman put his toga on, as they were very long and heavy.

Step 1
The toga was a 5.5 m (18 ft) long semi-circular woollen sheet. Different colours of toga were used for different occasions. After you have put on your tunic, pick your toga.

Step 2
Drape one end of the toga over your arm and shoulder, making sure the fabric reaches the floor. Then wind the other end around your back.

Step 3
Pass the toga under your arm and back over the first shoulder again. Be careful not to let the fabric on your first arm slide off.

Step 4
Make sure the toga is secure. Now you're properly dressed and ready to go!

Roman baths

Every Roman town had a bathhouse for the local people. This was not just a place to wash, but also to exercise, relax, and meet friends. Men and women bathed separately. Big baths had separate areas for men and women. With smaller baths, men and women went at different times of day.

HOW TO USE THE BATHS

A **Apodyterium** Romans went to the changing rooms (apodyterium) first to undress. Slaves guarded any valuables.

B **Palaestra** Visitors might then go to the palaestra, an area for exercise. People used lead weights, wrestled, or played ball games to work up a sweat.

C **Natatio** They could then take a swim in the (unheated) swimming pool, called a natatio.

D **Tepidarium** In the warm room, slaves would rub visitors with scented oil, and use a curved bronze tool called a strigil to scrape away dirt and dead skin.

E **Caldarium** Romans might visit the hot room (caldarium) next to sit in the steam bath. This was heated with hot air flowing under the floor.

F **Frigidarium** People visited the cold room (frigidarium) and jumped into a refreshing plunge bath to cool off.

Tepidarium
People often returned to the warm room at the end to relax and for a final rub with oil.

Furnace
The baths were heated by hot air from a furnace. Slaves brought a constant supply of wood to feed the fire. The hottest room was the one nearest the furnace.

Hypocaust
The floor rested on columns of brick, creating spaces for hot air from the furnace to pass through. This underfloor heating system is called a hypocaust.

Apodyterium
There were openings in the walls of the changing room for visitors to leave their clothes.

Frigidarium
This cold room, with its plunge pool, is the one furthest away from the furnace.

Baths at Bath

The Romans built this bathhouse in the city of Bath in England, taking advantage of a natural supply of hot water. The baths were sacred to a goddess called Sulis Minerva.

The Great Bath, Bath, England

Eat like a Roman

Rich Romans loved to throw dinner parties, where they served course after course of unusual dishes. We can still read Roman cookbooks, which have recipes for flamingo tongues, ostrich brains, and boiled parrots!

Snails
Snails were such a popular food that they were raised on special snail farms, where they were fed on milk.

Garlic
The Romans liked garlic for its taste and because they thought it gave them strength. Roman soldiers ate garlic before going into battle.

Fruit
Romans enjoyed fresh fruit for dessert. They ate many types of fruit, including figs and pears.

Oysters

Oysters were eaten by rich and poor. Vast numbers of oyster shells have been found in Roman rubbish dumps.

Fish

The Romans ate all kinds of fish. They also loved a spicy sauce, called garum, made from the rotting insides of mackerel and other fish.

I hear they eat flamingos ...I'm getting out of here!

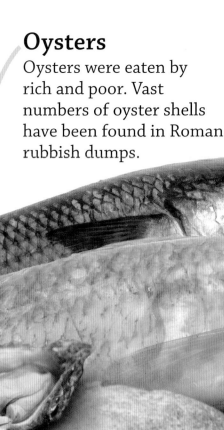

Bread

Bread was the main food eaten every day by the poor. Loaves of Roman bread have been found in the ruins of Herculaneum, near Pompeii.

Dormice

Dormice were fattened up in special pottery jars before being eaten. A baked stuffed dormouse was a popular snack.

Olives

The Romans ate olives whole, but they also pressed them to make olive oil. This oil was used in cooking and burned in lamps.

Dinner party

This Roman painting shows the end of a dinner party. Dinner, or cena, often lasted for hours and included entertainment like music and dancing. Romans ate and drank while lying on couches while slaves served food and drink. The food here has been cleared away and the guests are now drinking wine.

! WOW!

Romans ate with their **fingers**, though used a spoon for soup!

WHAT'S IN THE PICTURE?

1 **Wall painting** This painting is from a house in Pompeii.

2 **Triclinium** Roman dining rooms had three couches for guests to lie on. Only two can be seen here.

3 **Table** Food and drink was placed on low tables so it was within easy reach.

4 **Bowl** Diners washed their hands in bowls between each course.

5 **Wreaths** Rings of leaves were worn like party hats.

6 **Pale skin** This was fashionable for women and was a sign of high status (class).

7 **Wine** Romans added water to their wine to make it weaker.

8 **Tableware** Glass cups and bowls were expensive.

9 **Couch** Padded cushions made couches comfortable to recline on.

10 **Loose, light clothes** These were worn by the men, unlike the heavy toga worn in public. Their uncovered shoulders show they are relaxing.

Sage
This plant was sacred to the Romans. It was thought to have powerful healing properties.

Fenugreek seeds
Roman doctors prescribed seeds of the fenugreek plant for treating pneumonia.

Flax seeds
Crushed flax seeds were used to help heal wounds and soothe sore throats.

Black pepper
Medicines containing black pepper were used to treat many problems, including colds, earache and toothache.

Chamomile
This plant was used to treat headaches, as well as liver and kidney problems.

Hook retractor
A hook was used to hold blood vessels out of the way during operations.

Ligula
This bronze instrument, a ligula, could be used to mix and apply ointments or remove earwax.

Medicine

Roman doctors used many medicines, made from lots of different plants, to fight disease. The Romans were also skilled surgeons, thanks to years of experience treating wounded soldiers and gladiators. Alongside practical treatments, the sick prayed to the gods to help them get well.

34

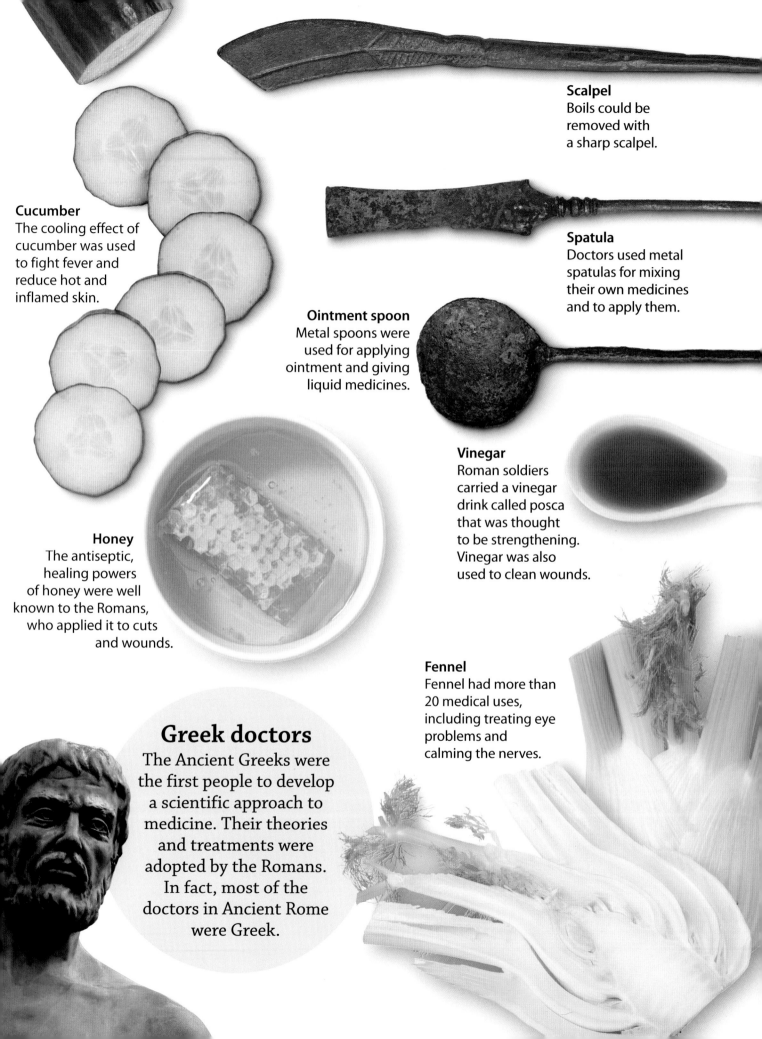

Scalpel
Boils could be removed with a sharp scalpel.

Cucumber
The cooling effect of cucumber was used to fight fever and reduce hot and inflamed skin.

Spatula
Doctors used metal spatulas for mixing their own medicines and to apply them.

Ointment spoon
Metal spoons were used for applying ointment and giving liquid medicines.

Vinegar
Roman soldiers carried a vinegar drink called posca that was thought to be strengthening. Vinegar was also used to clean wounds.

Honey
The antiseptic, healing powers of honey were well known to the Romans, who applied it to cuts and wounds.

Fennel
Fennel had more than 20 medical uses, including treating eye problems and calming the nerves.

Greek doctors
The Ancient Greeks were the first people to develop a scientific approach to medicine. Their theories and treatments were adopted by the Romans. In fact, most of the doctors in Ancient Rome were Greek.

Latin

Would you like to speak some Latin, the language of the Romans? We've labelled this town street with Latin words, and how to say them. In fact, you might already use Latin without knowing it. Many European languages still use letters and words similar to ones in Latin. Thousands of English words come from Roman ones.

Panis
(PAN-iss)
Bread

Tabula
(TAB-u-la)
Tablet

Thermopolium
(ther-mo-POLE-ee-um)
Snack bar

Puer
(POO-er)
Boy

Vir
(weer)
Man

Caput
(CAP-oot)
Head

Brachium
(BRAK-ee-um)
Arm

Crus
(croos)
Leg

Manus
(MAN-oos)
Hand

Via
(WEE-ah)
Street

Calx
(KAL-ix)
Heel

Genu
(GAY-noo)
Knee

Columna
(col-OOM-na)
Column

Ianua
(YAN-oo-ah)
Front door

Miles
(MEE-lays)
Soldier

Pisces
(PIE-sees)
Fish

Cave canem

A mosaic is a picture made up of tiny squares of stone or glass. This one shows a dog and the words "Cave canem". Can you guess what the Latin words mean? They say, "Beware of the dog".

Mosaic found in the city of Pompeii.

Fenestra
(fen-ESS-tra)
Window

Puella
(POO-el-ah)
Girl

Corbis
(KOR-biss)
Basket

Mendicus
(MEN-di-koos)
Beggar

Domina
(DOM-ee-nah)
Woman

Maleus
(MAL-ee-oos)
Hammer

Canis
(CAN-iss)
Dog

J. Williamson

37

Roman numbers

The Romans used letters to stand for numbers, such as V for 5. We call these letters Roman numerals. Roman numerals were used throughout the Roman Empire for counting and pricing goods. Even after the end of the Empire, the numerals continued to be used throughout Europe for hundreds of years.

FACT FILE

» **Seven symbols**
Roman numerals have 7 symbols:

I = 1

V = 5

X = 10

L = 50

C = 100

D = 500

M = 1,000

How numerals worked

The Romans only used seven letters to make all their numbers. Each has a set value, such as X for 10. Numbers without a matching letter are made by adding or subtracting the values of these seven letters. If a smaller numeral is to the right of a larger one, you add them, so LX stands for 60 (50 + 10). But if the smaller numeral is to the left of the bigger one, we take the smaller one away. So 40 is shown by XL (50 - 10).

! WOW!

The Romans had **no numeral** for **zero!**

1	2	3
4	5	6
7	8	9
10	20	30
40	50	60
70	80	90
100	500	1000

Numerals now

Although Roman numerals are quite complicated, we still use them for decoration. Look out for Roman numerals on clock faces, coins, and on the dates at the end of television programmes.

Alarm clock

Big numbers

To work out a big number written in Roman numerals, first list the 1000s, then the 100s, then the 10s, and last the 1s. Finally, add them together.

For example, **MMXVI** is

M   M   X   V   I

1000 + 1000 + 10 + 5 + 1

= 2016

I   II   III

IV   V   VI

VII   VIII   IX

X   XX   XXX

XL   L   LX

LXX   LXXX   XC

C   D   M

Crack the code

Complete these sums on a piece of paper then add up the answers to find out which year Pompeii was destroyed by the eruption of Mount Vesuvius. The answer is at the bottom of the page.

X + VII = ?

L - XX = ?

C ÷ V = ?

X + II = ?

Now add up your answers!

Today, we can turn a 3 into 30 by adding a zero. But the Romans couldn't do this. To write 30, they wrote the symbol for ten – X – three times.

2

4

7

City of Rome

This is a model of the centre of Rome, capital city of the Empire. It was full of grand public buildings including temples, law courts, and sports arenas. Rome was also home to the emperor, whose huge palace stood on the Palatine Hill.

WHAT'S IN THE PICTURE?

1 **The Forum** The centre of government, law, and business.

2 **Circus Maximus** The Empire's greatest racetrack, used for chariot racing.

3 **Capitoline Hill** Rome's most important temples stood on this hill. The biggest one was the Temple of Jupiter.

4 **Palatine Hill** This hilltop was covered with palaces, built by several emperors.

5 **The Temple of Claudius** Temple named after Claudius, who was declared a god after he died.

6 **The Colosseum** This open-air building was used for gladiator fights.

7 **The Aqua Claudia** One of eleven great aqueducts, bringing water to the city.

Building work

Roman builders copied the styles of Greek architecture, but built on a much grander scale. They made great use of arches, mass-produced bricks and concrete, and built the world's first domes. The Romans were so good at building that many of their aqueducts, temples, and bridges are still standing.

Arch

A building with arches is as strong as one with solid walls, but is much quicker to build. The Romans used arches to build this aqueduct (bridge for carrying water) across a French river.

Pont du Gard, France

Insula

Town buildings were divided into blocks, called insulae (islands). The brick apartments of insulae could be up to seven storeys high.

Insula in Herculaneum

Wall

A lot of building work was done by the Roman army. They built Hadrian's Wall to form a defensive barrier that separated the Romans in Britannia from the tribes further north.

Hadrian's Wall, England

Insula in Ostia, Rome

Dome

The Romans invented the dome, a rounded roof used to span a wide space. This is the concrete dome of the Pantheon, a temple to all the gods built by Emperor Hadrian in Rome.

Temple

Roman temples look like Greek temples. But while the Greeks built using cut stone, the Romans used cheaper bricks. They saved stone for the facings (decorative features). Temples were used to honour gods, and some even honoured emperors.

Temple of Bacchus, Lebanon

Column

In Rome, Emperor Trajan built a 38 m (125 ft) high marble column, decorated with scenes of his wars of conquest. His ashes were buried in the base.

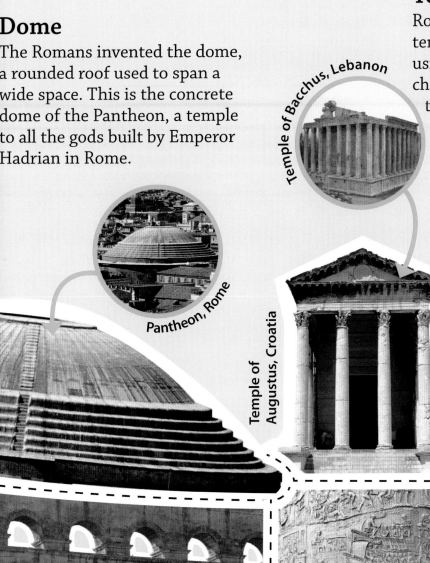

Pantheon, Rome

Temple of Augustus, Croatia

Trajan's Column, Rome

Road

The Roman Army also built a network of long straight roads, with deep foundations. These were the best roads built until modern times. One of the most important roads they built was the Appian Way (Via Appia Antica).

Via Appia Antica, Rome

The Colosseum

The Colosseum in Rome was the Empire's biggest amphitheatre, a building for open-air shows. It seated 50,000 visitors, who came to watch men, called gladiators, and wild animals fighting and being killed for entertainment.

WHAT'S IN THE COLOSSEUM?

A **Imperial box** The emperor and his family sat in a big box in the front row.

B **Lowest level** The richest male citizens sat in the lowest level, where they had the best view.

C **Middle level** Ordinary male citizens sat in the second level.

D **Highest level** The highest level was for women and foreign visitors to Rome.

E **Arena** The arena, or fighting area, had a wooden floor covered with sand to soak up blood.

F **Gladiators' entrance** The show began with a parade by the gladiators, who entered through this gateway.

G **Statues** The outer walls were decorated with statues of gods and emperors.

Entrances
There were 80 street entrances to the Colosseum so the audience could enter and exit quickly.

Fight to the death
Gladiators fought in pairs or against animals. They often fought to the death.

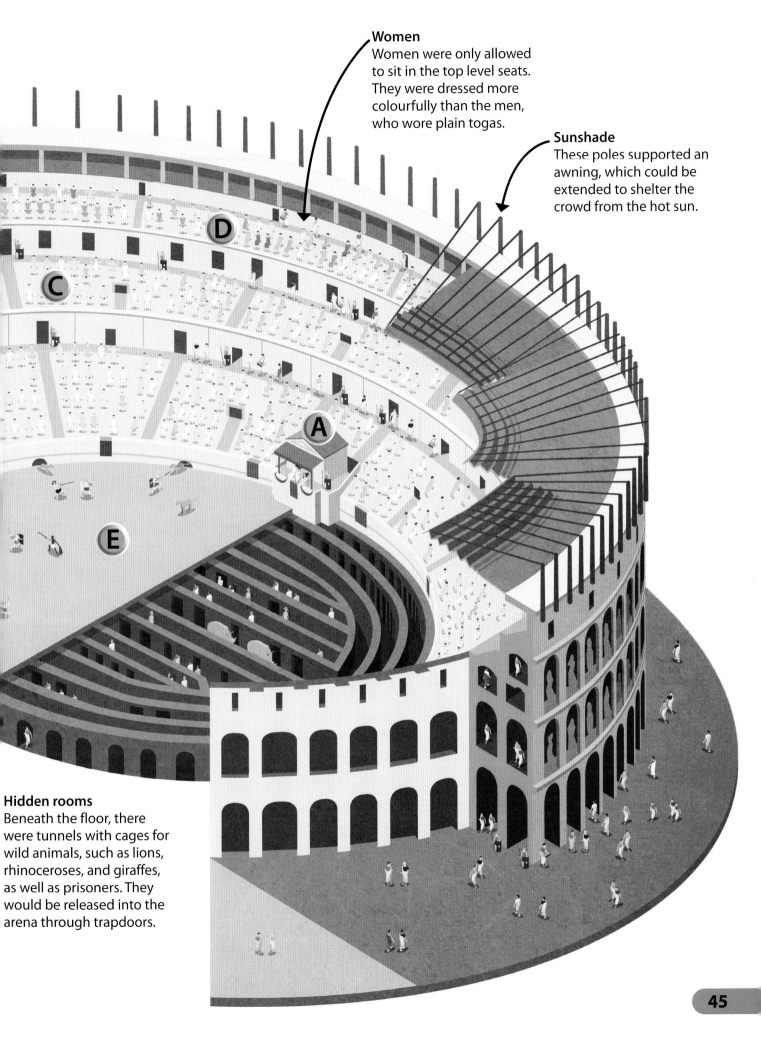

Women
Women were only allowed to sit in the top level seats. They were dressed more colourfully than the men, who wore plain togas.

Sunshade
These poles supported an awning, which could be extended to shelter the crowd from the hot sun.

Hidden rooms
Beneath the floor, there were tunnels with cages for wild animals, such as lions, rhinoceroses, and giraffes, as well as prisoners. They would be released into the arena through trapdoors.

Gladiators

Romans loved watching shows in which gladiators fought to the death. Most gladiators were slaves, convicted criminals, or prisoners of war, who were forced to fight. However, some free men, who liked fighting and sought the fame and wealth success brought, chose to be gladiators. There were several types, each armed in different ways.

PROVOCATOR

Weapons
Gladius (short sword)

Armour
Helmet, breastplate, tall shield, right arm guard, left shin guard

Special features
The provocator (challenger) was the only gladiator to wear a breastplate. He usually fought other provocators.

MURMILLO

Weapons
Gladius (short sword)

Armour
Big helmet, tall shield, right arm guard, left shin guard

Special features
The murmillo (fish man) had a tall helmet, often decorated with a fish crest. He was a slow, heavily armoured fighter.

RETIARIUS

Weapons
Trident (fishing spear), net, and dagger

Armour
Right shoulder and arm guard

Special features
The retiarius (net man) was armed like a fisherman, with a net to trap his opponent and a trident. With little armour, he had to move very quickly.

SECUTOR

 Weapons
Gladius
(short sword)

 Armour
Rounded helmet,
tall shield, right
arm guard, left
shin guard

Special features
The secutor
(pursuer) always
fought against a
retiarius. His helmet
was rounded,
making it harder
to get caught in
the retiarius's net.

5 AMAZING FACTS

Gladiators

1 **Gladiator** means "sword man", from the gladius (short sword) that most gladiators carried.

2 **Women** also became gladiators. A female fighter was called a gladiatrix.

3 **Successful gladiators** were treated like today's pop stars.

4 **Famous fights** were pictured on the walls of fans' houses.

5 **Wild animals** were fought by gladiators called bestiarii.

THRAEX

Weapons
Curved sword

 Armour
Helmet, small
shield, thigh-length
leg guards

 Special features
The equipment
of the Thraex
(also known as
a Thracian), was
based on that used
by the Thracians,
who were
long-standing
enemies of Rome.

HOPLOMACHUS

Weapons
Gladius (short
sword) and spear

Armour
Feather-topped
helmet, round
shield, right arm
guard, thigh-length
leg guards

Special features
The hoplomachus
("armed fighter"
in Greek) had the
round shield and
spear of a Greek
foot-soldier.

In the arena!

It's the day of the games, and Memnon, the murmillo, is due to fight Felix, the retiarius. Memnon has never yet lost a fight, but he's getting older and slower. Felix has less experience, but he's young and fit. Who will win today?

RETIARIUS

MURMILLO

WE WHO ARE ABOUT TO DIE SALUTE YOU!

VS

Gladiators fought in pairs. The lightly armoured retiarius was often matched with heavily armoured murmillo.

The summa rudis (referee) raises his staff, and orders the fight to begin.

OOOF!

Felix rushes forward with his long trident, hoping to take Memnon by surprise. His trident bounces off Memnon's shield.

Memnon now attacks back. He strikes at Felix, but catches his shoulder guard. The summa rudis watches on.

POW!

Racing track

Welcome to Rome's main chariot-racing track: the Circus Maximus! Chariot racing was an exciting and dangerous sport. A chariot was a horse-drawn cart whose driver was called a charioteer. Charioteers were grouped into four teams: the Reds, Whites, Blues, and Greens. Each team had loyal fans, who cheered as the chariots hurtled around the track.

Chariot

This model chariot is made of metal. To be as fast as possible, real chariots were made of light wood. They gave no protection to a charioteer if he crashed.

Chariots had two wheels.

Spectators
There was seating for 250,000 people, five times more than the Colosseum could hold. Men and women sat together.

(A)

Biggest circus!
Circus Maximus is Latin for "biggest circus". It was 621 m (2,037 ft) long and 118 m (387 ft) wide.

The turn
The most dangerous part of any chariot race was the point where the chariots had to turn. They often crashed into each other or overturned here.

Arcades
In the long arcades facing the street, there were stalls selling snacks and drinks. Fortune tellers also set up stalls here.

Track
Chariots raced seven times around the track. The winner was the first chariot to complete all seven laps.

WHAT'S IN THE CIRCUS MAXIMUS?

A **Carceres** Chariots raced out of these starting gates at the beginning of a race.

B **Quadriga** Chariot pulled by four horses.

C **Lap markers** Seven bronze dolphins and seven wooden eggs were used to mark the laps. After each lap, a dolphin was turned around and an egg removed.

D **Pulvinar** Imperial box, where the emperor and his family and friends sat.

E **Egyptian obelisk** Four-sided, pointed pillar, brought to Rome by Emperor Augustus.

F **Spina** Barrier down the middle of the track. It was decorated with statues and other monuments.

G **Metae** Three tall posts at either end of the spina marked the turning point for the chariots.

Answer our quiz to find out which Roman god or goddess you are.

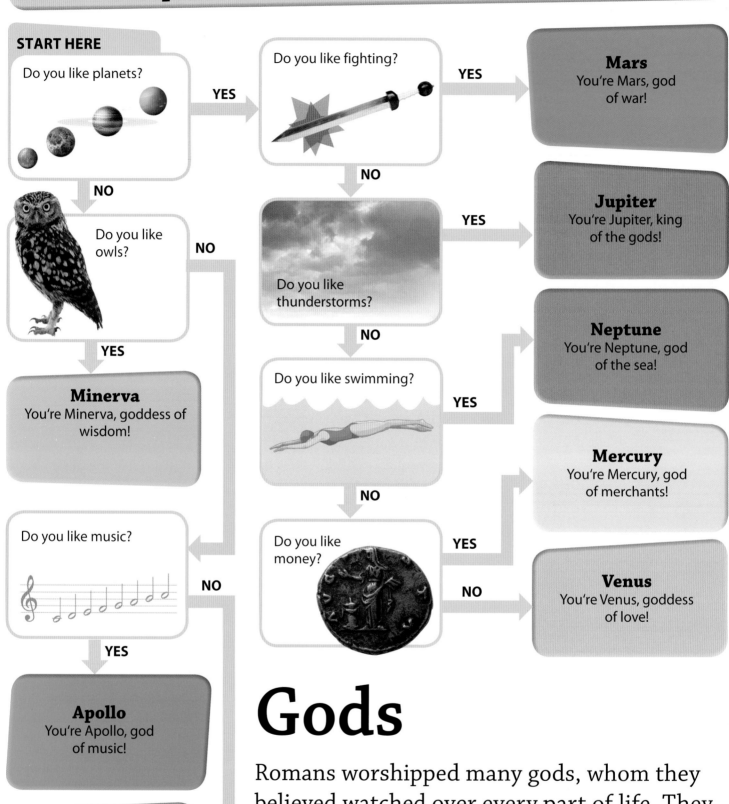

START HERE

Do you like planets?

YES → Do you like fighting? **YES** → **Mars** You're Mars, god of war!

NO ↓

Do you like owls? **NO** →

Do you like fighting? **NO** ↓

Do you like thunderstorms? **YES** → **Jupiter** You're Jupiter, king of the gods!

Do you like owls? **YES** ↓

Minerva You're Minerva, goddess of wisdom!

Do you like thunderstorms? **NO** ↓

Do you like swimming? **YES** → **Neptune** You're Neptune, god of the sea!

Do you like swimming? → **Mercury** You're Mercury, god of merchants!

Do you like swimming? **NO** ↓

Do you like money? **YES** → (Mercury)

Do you like money? **NO** → **Venus** You're Venus, goddess of love!

Do you like music? **NO** →

Do you like music? **YES** ↓

Apollo You're Apollo, god of music!

Juno You're Juno, queen of the gods!

Gods

Romans worshipped many gods, whom they believed watched over every part of life. They ranged from great ones, whom they built great temples for, down to household gods who guarded the home.

Mercury

Mercury was the god of merchants, money, and travellers. He travelled fast, thanks to his winged hat and sandals. He also carried a staff called the caduceus that had two snakes wrapped around it.

Jupiter

Jupiter was king of the gods and special protector of the Roman Empire. He was god of the sky and storms, and was armed with thunderbolts. The eagle was his sacred bird.

Juno

Jupiter's wife, Juno, was the goddess of marriage and childbirth. Her sacred bird was the peacock. The Roman month of Junius (June), was named after her, and was thought a lucky time to marry.

Minerva

Minerva was the goddess of crafts and wisdom. She was born from Jupiter's head, complete with her armour and weapons. Her sacred bird was the wise owl.

Mars

Mars was the god of war and also of farming. After Jupiter, he was the most important Roman god. The Roman month Martius (March) is named after him.

Neptune

Jupiter's brother, Neptune, was the god of the sea and horses. Armed with a trident (fishing spear), he rode in a chariot pulled by fish-tailed horses called hippocamps.

Apollo

Apollo was the god of light, healing, music, and prophecy (telling the future). He played a musical instrument called a lyre, that Mercury invented.

Venus

Venus was the goddess of love and beauty. Julius Caesar claimed Venus was one of his ancestors. The month of Aprilis (April) was sacred to her.

! WOW!

There was a goddess, called **Cardea**, who looked after **door hinges!**

Pompeii

Mount Vesuvius today

On 24 August 79CE, Mount Vesuvius, a volcano in southern Italy, blew up, completely burying the nearby town of Pompeii. Although it was a terrible disaster, the town was perfectly preserved by being buried. This means that we can now explore the streets, houses, and shops of a Roman town.

The Forum of Pompeii

Victims of Pompeii

Apart from buildings, some of the victims who died at Pompeii almost 2,000 years ago were discovered. Their bodies were buried in ash from the eruption, which turned to rock around them. After they had rotted away, plaster was poured into the spaces they left to create casts.

Dog with collar

Dog
This is the cast of a guard dog. You can see the outline of its collar, which was made from bronze.

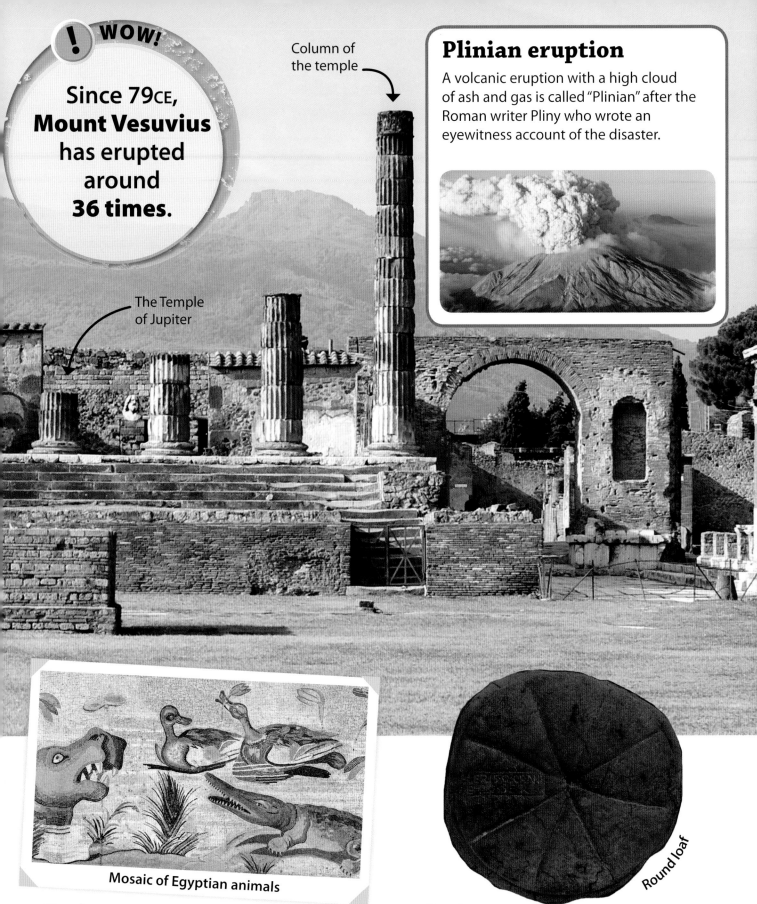

Column of the temple

Plinian eruption

A volcanic eruption with a high cloud of ash and gas is called "Plinian" after the Roman writer Pliny who wrote an eyewitness account of the disaster.

The Temple of Jupiter

Mosaic of Egyptian animals

Round loaf

Mosaic
The houses of Pompeii were richly decorated with wall paintings and mosaics. This mosaic shows a hippopotamus and a crocodile.

Bread
This loaf of bread was found in a baker's oven in Herculaneum, Pompeii's neighbouring town. It was preserved by boiling mud.

What did the Romans give us?

The Roman Empire fell in the fifth century CE, following invasions by foreign enemies. But even today, 1,500 years later, Rome still has an influence. We still travel along the routes of Roman roads, and coins and many buildings are based on Roman ones.

Lost and found

Concrete, now used everywhere in building, was invented by the Romans. Roman concrete was better than any made today, but the recipe got lost!

Glass

The Romans were expert glass-makers. They used it to make drinking vessels, vases, and jugs. They were also the first people to use glass in windows.

This glass jug was found in Kent, England.

! WOW!

The Romans even invented books with pages!

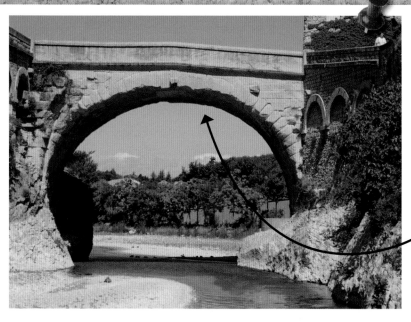

Bridges

The Romans built some of the first permanent bridges. They were made from stone, brick, and concrete, and used single or multiple arches.

This Roman bridge across the Ouveze river in France is still in use today, despite being 2,000 years old.

Roman writers

Although the Roman Empire ended many years ago, we can still read the writings of Roman poets like Virgil. Virgil was seen by the Romans as their greatest poet.

This mosaic shows Virgil writing the *Aeneid*, his most famous poem.

12

Twelve-month calendar

Our 12 month calendar is Roman. Most of our months are named after Roman numbers and gods, such as March, named after the god Mars. However, July and August are named after Julius Caesar and Emperor Augustus.

Alphabet

Our alphabet is mostly a Roman invention. However, the Romans had 23 letters while we now have 26, and they only used capital letters. They would have written Julius as IVLIVS.

Roman alphabet

ABCDEF GHIKLM NOPQR STVXYZ

Can you see which 3 letters are missing?

Answer: J, U, W

Cities

Across Europe, we live in cities founded by the Romans. As well as Rome in Italy (above), Roman cities include London and York in the UK, Paris and Lyons in France, Cordoba and Seville in Spain, and Cologne in Germany.

Roman facts and figures

The Romans were a fascinating group of people. Here are some amazing facts you might not know about them!

The mythical founder of Rome, Romulus, and his brother, Remus, were said to have been **raised by a wolf.**

HAIRY TRUTH!

There were people in Rome who earned their living by plucking other people's hair out, including their armpit hair!

52BCE Vercingetorix, a chieftain from Gaul (France), fought a war against Julius Caesar, but lost. He was led in chains through Rome in Julius Caesar's victory procession.

Constantine
was the first Christian emperor: he didn't worship the Roman gods.

50 400,000

Around 50 of today's countries were part of the Roman Empire.

The Romans built 400,000 km (250,000 miles) of roads.

ROME WAS RULED BY EMPERORS FOR OVER

400
YEARS.

ROMAN SOLDIERS had to serve for **25 years** in the army. They could walk up to **30 km (20 miles) a day** wearing heavy armour.

Romans made purple dye for clothes from
SEA SNAIL SHELLS.

Romans used a two-handed jar called an
AMPHORA
to store all sorts of goods, such as olive oil, wine, and even garum (fish sauce).

7
Rome was ruled by seven kings before it became a republic.

117
Hadrian's Wall was 117 km (73 miles) long.

100
The opening games for the Colosseum lasted for more than 100 days.

Glossary

Here are the meanings of some words that are useful for you to know when learning about Ancient Rome.

abacus Device with moveable beads, used by the Romans to count

amphitheatre Big, oval, open-air building used for public shows, especially gladiator fights

amphora Two-handled jar, used by the Romans to store food, drinks, and oil

aqueduct Artificial channel used to carry water to a town

auxillary Member of the Roman army who was not a Roman citizen

bulla Amulet worn by Roman boys that was thought to protect them

centurion Roman soldier in charge of 80 legionaries

chariot Two-wheeled vehicle pulled by horses, used by the Romans for racing

circus Roman racetrack, for chariot racing

citizen Member of a state, with more rights than a non-citizen

civil war War fought between people who belong to the same country.

dictator Ruler with total power. Under the republic, dictators were appointed in times of emergency. But Julius Caesar made himself dictator for life

dome Large, rounded roof or ceiling with a circular base

emperor Ruler of an empire

empire Large area with different peoples, ruled by a single government or person

forum Central market-place and public meeting area in every Roman town

freedmen and freedwomen Former slaves who bought or were given their freedom

garum Rotten fish sauce, eaten by the Romans

gladiator Type of fighter who entertained people by fighting in an amphitheatre. Gladiators were usually slaves

Roman aqueduct

insula Roman block of flats

Latin Language of the Romans

legion Roman army of around 5,000 citizen soldiers. The Roman Empire had between 25 and 30 of them

legionary Roman foot soldier, who was the basic unit of the Roman army

mosaic Picture made of many tiny pieces of coloured tile, stone, or glass, pushed into cement

palla Shawl worn by Roman women

Roman women wore a stola (dress) and palla (shawl).

republic State ruled by elected officials instead of a king or emperor. The term is also used to describe the period, between 509–27BCE, when Rome was ruled by elected officials

Roman Empire Lands and peoples ruled by the Romans. The term is also used to describe the period when Rome was ruled by emperors rather than by elected officials

Saturnalia Festival when masters served their slaves

Senate Roman governing council, made up of the most important Roman nobles. It gave advice to the emperor

slave Someone who is owned by another person as property

stola Dress worn by Roman women

stylus Pointed metal stick used to write on a tablet

summa rudis Referee in a gladiator fight

tablet Wooden frame filled with wax, used by children to practise writing

Roman men wore togas.

toga Woollen gown worn by Roman male citizens. It was made of a single sheet wrapped around the body

triclinium Roman dining room with three couches for guests to lie down on

tunic Item of clothing worn by all Romans, made from two squares of material sewn together

wreath Crown of leaves, sometimes worn by Roman emperors

Index

Acknowledgements

The publisher would like to thank the following people for their assistance: Cecile Landau and Ruth O'Rourke for editorial assistance, Alexandra Beeden for proofreading, Helen Peters for compiling the index, Rob Nunn for picture research, Lol Johnson for photography, Sachin Singh for cutouts, and Daniel Long, Dan Crisp, and Ed Merritt for illustrations. The publishers would also like to thank the Roman and Barbarian warriors from Britannia (www.durolitum.co.uk) and the Gallic chieftan and auxilliary soldier from Portals to the Past (www.portalstothepast.co.uk).

The publisher would like to thank the following for their kind permission to reproduce their photographs:

(Key: a-above; b-below/bottom; c-centre; f-far; l-left; r-right; t-top)

2 Rex Shutterstock: De Agostini / A. Dagli Orti (br). 3 Alamy Images: A. Astes (bl). Dorling Kindersley: Thackeray Medical Museum (bc); The University of Aberdeen (tr). 4-5 Alamy Images: Fine Art Images / Heritage Image Partnership Ltd. 11 Alamy Images: A. Astes (l). Dorling Kindersley: Ermine Street Guard (br). 12 Alamy Images: Lanmas (cra). Dorling Kindersley: Capitoline Museum, Rome (Musei Capitolini) (cl). 13 Alamy Images: Masterpics (tr). 14-15 Alamy Images: EmmePi Travel. 17 Dorling Kindersley: Ermine Street Guard (br). 18 Alamy Images: Michele Falzone (bl). Dorling Kindersley: Christi Graham and Nick Nicholls / The Trustees of the British Museum (ftr, ca). Rex Shutterstock: De Agostini / A. Dagli Orti (cl). 19 Dorling Kindersley: Odds Farm Park, High Wycombe, Bucks (clb); Thackeray Medical Museum (cr). Getty Images: Danita Delimont / Gallo Images (c). 20 Dorling Kindersley: Christi Graham and Nick Nicholls / The Trustees of the British Museum (tl, ca). 21 Corbis: Wolfgang Kaehler (b). 22 Photoshot: UPPA (br). 24 Alamy Images: Collection Dagli Orti / The Art Archive (tl). Bridgeman Images: Tarker (cr). Dorling Kindersley: Maidstone Museum and Bentliff Art Gallery (c). 25 Alamy Images: Lanmas (tr); World History Archive (tl). Dorling Kindersley: Tim Parmenter / The Trustees of the British Museum (cl); The Science Museum, London (cla). Getty Images: DEA Picture Library / De Agostini Picture Library (br); DEA / G. Dagli Orti / De Agostini Picture Library (fcl). 29 Alamy Images: Peter Phipp / Travelshots.com (cra). 32-33 Corbis: Alessandra Benedetti. 34 Dorling Kindersley: Thackeray Medical Museum (br, fbr). 35 Alamy Images: Milleflore Images - Food and Tableware Misc (fcr); Bruce Miller (bl). Dorling Kindersley: Thackeray Medical Museum (tr, cra, cr). 36-37 Alamy Images: Lebrecht Music and Arts Photo Library. 37 Alamy Images: Gianni Dagli Orti / The Art Archive (cra). 38 Alamy Images: Art Nation (br). 39 Alamy Images: geogphotos (br). 40-41 Alamy Images: Lautaro. 42 Alamy Images: Granger, NYC (cb); Prisma Archivo (c); Stephen Dorey Creative (clb). Dorling Kindersley: Tim Draper / Rough Guides (cl). 42-43 Getty Images: DEA / S. Vannini / De Agostini (b). 43 Alamy Images: Reinhard Dirscherl (cl, cla); imageBROKER (cr). 46-47 Alamy Images: Aliaksei Verasovich. 52 Dorling Kindersley: Ermine Street Guard (tc). 54 Alamy Images: Walter Rawlings / robertharding (br). 54-55 Alamy Images: Vaclav Schindler. 55 Alamy Images: funkyfood London - Paul Williams (bl). Corbis: Gary Braasch (tr). Dorling Kindersley: Museo Archeologico Nazionale di Napoli (br). 56 Alamy Images: David A. Barnes (bl). Dorling Kindersley: Canterbury City Council, Museums and Galleries (cl). 57 Alamy Images: Sergey Borisov (clb). Corbis: Roger Wood (cla). 58 Dorling Kindersley: Thackeray Medical Museum (ca); Jerry Young (fcl). Dreamstime.com: Vladimir Korostyshevskiy / v0v (cr). Getty Images: De Agostini / L. Romano / De Agostini Picture Library (br). 59 Dorling Kindersley: The University of Aberdeen (tc). Endpapers: Front: Alamy Images: funkyfood London - Paul Williams (trajan); Massimiliano Pieraccini (constatine). Dorling Kindersley: The Trustees of the British Museum (coin); Tim Draper / Rough Guides (wall). Back: Alamy Images: Ian Bottle (hadrian's wall); Martin Garnham (rotunda of galerius); Amar and Isabelle Guillen - Guillen Photo LLC (kom el-dikka); Andrey Nekrasov (amphitheatre of thysdrus); OlegMit (pompeii); Stefano Politi Markovina (library of celsus); Premier (leptis magna); Michael Runkel / imageBROKER (ruins of djemila); Juergen Schonnop (pont du gard); Vivienne Sharp / Imagestate Media Partners Limited - Impact Photos (temple of bacchus); Claude Thibault (tower of hercules). Corbis: Marco Cristofori (diocletian's palace).

Cover images: Front: Corbis: Araldo de Luca cl; Dorling Kindersley: The University of Aberdeen fcra; Getty Images: Danita Delimont / Gallo Images cr; Back: Dorling Kindersley: Ermine Street Guard cla, cr; Rex by Shutterstock: De Agostini / A. Dagli Orti tr

All other images © Dorling Kindersley
For further information see:
www.dkimages.com

About the author

Peter Chrisp is an experienced author, who has published more than 80 books on history for young readers. His special interest is in the Ancient World, and he is the author of a number of Dorling Kindersley books, including *Ancient Rome Revealed, Ancient Greece Revealed, E. Explore: Ancient Rome, E. Explore: Ancient Greece,* and *Alexander the Great: Legend of a Warrior King.*